The
North
American
Indians

The
Navajo

Titles in The North American Indians series include:

The North American Indians

The Navajo

P.M. Boekhoff and Stuart A. Kallen

KIDHAVEN
PRESS™

THOMSON
★
GALE

San Diego • Detroit • New York • San Francisco • Cleveland
New Haven, Conn. • Waterville, Maine • London • Munich

© 2004 by KidHaven Press. KidHaven Press is an imprint of The Gale Group, Inc., a division of Thomson Learning, Inc.

KidHaven™ and Thomson Learning™ are trademarks used herein under license.

For more information, contact
KidHaven Press
27500 Drake Rd.
Farmington Hills, MI 48331-3535
Or you can visit our Internet site at http://www.gale.com

LIBRARY OF CONGRESS CATALOGING-IN-PUBLICATION DATA

Boekhoff, P.M. (Patti Marlene), 1957–
  The Navajo / by P.M. Boekhoff & Stuart A. Kallen.
    p. cm. — (The North American Indians)
  Summary: Discusses the Navajo people, their customs, family, organizations, food gathering, religion, war, housing, and other aspects of daily life.
  Includes bibliographical references and index.
   ISBN 0-7377-1512-X (alk. paper)
   1. Navajo Indians—Juvenile literature. [1. Navajo Indians. 2. Indians of North America—Southwest, New.] I. Kallen, Stuart A., 1955– II. Title. III. Series.
  E99.N3B58 2004
  979.1004'972—dc21

                                              2004007300

Contents

Chapter One

North to South

The Navajo have a long and exciting history in North America. It began in the frozen wilderness of Canada and continues today in the beautiful deserts of the American Southwest. Of all the Native American tribes in the United States, the Navajo is the largest, with about 250,000 members. The Navajo are closely related to the Apache, and both tribes moved from northwestern Canada to their present homeland along the Arizona-New Mexico border about five hundred years ago. While the Apache continued to wander throughout the region, the Navajo settled in an area already populated by tribes such as the Hopi, Taos, Zuni, and Tewa that together are known as the Pueblo.

The Navajo believed that their creators gave them the name Ni'hookaa Diyan Diné. This means "Holy Earth People" or "Lords of the Earth." The Navajo today simply call themselves "Diné," meaning "The People." The Tewa were the first to call them Navajo, which means "the large area of cultivated land."

From Rain Forest to Desert

The story of the Navajo begins in the Yukon region of northwestern Canada. In this frigid land of lush rain forests filled with ancient trees, the Navajo were **nomadic**, that is, they moved from place to place in search of food. They hunted with bows and arrows and found food and medicine in the wild plants that grow in woodlands, wetlands, and streams.

In addition to hunting, the Navajo built large fenced corrals and used these pens to hold wild elk and caribou. These animals were eaten, their bones made into tools, and their skins sewed into tepees, native tent-like homes. The Navajo also tamed other wild animals such as wolves that were taught to pull sleds through the deep Canadian winter snows.

It is unclear why the Navajo left their original homeland, but the tribe migrated far south to the Arizona

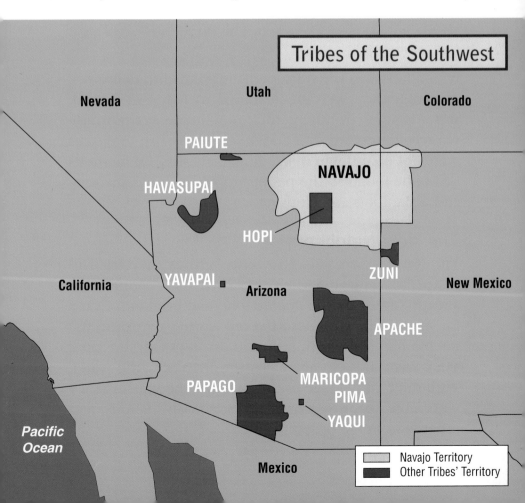

Tribes of the Southwest

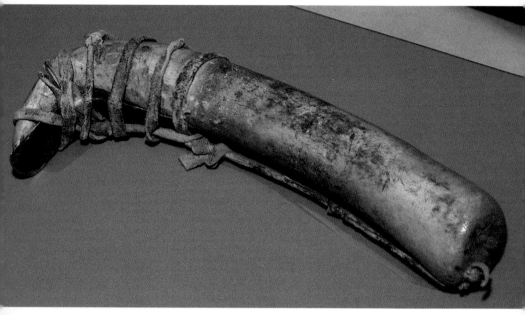

The Navajo used animal bones to make tools like this flesh scraper made from caribou bone.

region between the thirteenth and sixteenth centuries. Although they were accustomed to living in a cold, wet, forest environment, their new home in the south-western desert was hot and dry. Animals, fish, and trees were not plentiful in this region. New survival methods had to be found so the people could eat, build shelters, and make tools and clothing.

The New Neighbors

The Navajo were lucky to have help as they tried to **adapt** to their environment. Their new home was already settled by the Pueblo who had lived in the area for more than a thousand years. During that time the Pueblo had learned to farm the dry, rocky, desert land. They knew how to grow crops using very little water. With their knowledge of the land and the seasons, they were able to grow corn, beans, squash, melons, and other food in the desert.

The Navajo soon learned from their new neighbors how to survive and prosper. In Canada the Navajo had to travel long distances on sleds to find food. In the American Southwest they learned how to farm and grow enough food to stay in one place. As the years passed, the Navajo adopted Pueblo styles of weaving, fashion, and pottery as they built stable farming communities.

The New World

Soon after the Navajo moved to the Southwest, another group of newcomers arrived from Spain. These Europeans were explorers, soldiers, businessmen, missionaries, and settlers who brought an entirely new

A Spanish explorer rides his horse in the American Southwest. The Spanish taught the Navajo to ride horses, and the tribe became skilled horsemen.

culture to the Native Americans. The Navajo were very interested in trading with the Spanish and began exchanging food for guns and iron tools such as axes and knives.

As they had done with the Pueblo, the Navajo also adopted some of the farming practices of their Spanish neighbors. Native corn and bean crops were planted alongside European flax and wheat. Hunting for wild animals became less important as the Navajo began raising European farm animals such as horses, goats, sheep, and cows.

The introduction of livestock quickly changed the settled lives of the Navajo. By the early 1600s the Navajo had learned to ride horses, and before long the Navajo were skilled horsemen often able to outride Spanish soldiers.

Horses enabled tribes to travel through a much wider territory and were used by herders to drive large flocks of sheep into the cool mountains in the summertime. Horses also helped the Navajo travel great distances to trade. Many families collected buffalo robes, blankets, silver jewelry, bridles, and bits through successful trade.

Horses also allowed Navajo warriors to raid the villages of their Pueblo and Spanish neighbors. The Spanish fought back fiercely and conducted violent military raids against the Navajo, often taking prisoners and selling them into slavery.

Great Conflict

The clashes between the Navajo, Spanish, and Pueblo caused great disruption in tribal society. Spanish priests conquered the weakened Pueblo, took over their villages, built **missions**, and converted them to Christianity. The Spanish also forced the Pueblo into slavery, making them care for their animals, crops, and houses. The Navajo, however, were able to avoid much of this Spanish influence because they lived on small farms spread out over a wide area of the countryside.

A Spanish priest instructs Native Americans about the importance of the cross. Because the Navajo lived on isolated farms, they escaped the religious influence of the Spanish.

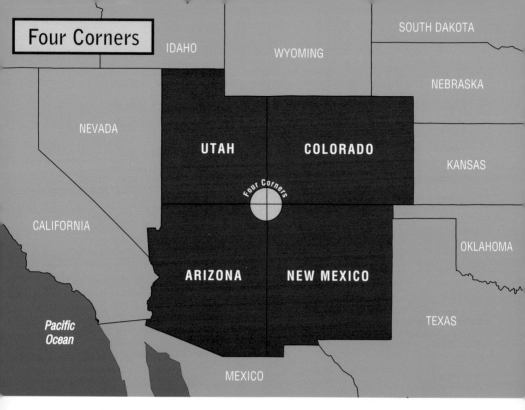

The Pueblo rebelled against slavery in 1680. They killed many Spanish people and drove the rest to the South. The Navajo captured much of the escaped Spanish livestock and moved north with it to the area known as Four Corners where the present-day states of Arizona, New Mexico, Colorado, and Utah come together. The Spanish soon returned with bigger armies and drove the Pueblo north onto this land. Now living in the same area, the Navajo and Pueblo tribes struggled to live in harmony.

A Mixing of Cultures

Although there were conflicts between the tribes, the Navajo continued to learn from their neighbors. For example, in the late seventeenth century Navajo women adopted the Pueblo method of weaving beautiful blankets and rugs. By adapting to new conditions and adopting the practices and the people of other cultures, the Navajo tribe grew and expanded in their new homeland in Four Corners.

Chapter Two

Family Life

Daily life among the Navajo is centered on home and family. Throughout the 1800s most people were married between the ages of fifteen and eighteen, and divorce among the Navajo was rare.

When a Navajo man wanted to marry, he would try to impress a woman with his hunting skills. To do so he would lay a freshly killed deer outside the door of her house. If the family was willing to have him as a son-in-law, the deer was taken in and eaten.

After marriage most young couples started a family. When a Navajo woman was about to give birth, her husband built a small, flat baby bed called a cradleboard to which the infant could be strapped. Using the cradleboard Navajo mothers carried their babies with them on their backs every day as they worked on their farms. Cradleboards could also be worn on the front so that the mother could talk to the baby and the baby could gaze into her eyes. In this way a mother and her child stayed close all day.

Couples did not live on their own but stayed with the wife's family, which might include parents, grandparents, aunts and uncles, and brothers and sisters. Everyone helped raise the children, and young boys and girls spent many hours learning about life from their aunts, uncles, and grandparents.

Navajo Clans

Like most other Native American tribes in the United States, the Navajo are still organized into extended fami-

A Navajo medicine man treats a woman and her child. The Navajo baby is strapped to a cradleboard.

A Navajo clan gathers for a meeting. The clan system maintained peace and order in tribal families and is still in use today.

lies called clans. Each clan has its own name, each with a special meaning to its members. Some of the many Navajo clan names include Deer People, Sticking-Up-Ears People, Many Mules Clan, Blue Bird People, and Near the Mountain Clan.

In the clan system, still in use today, tribe members trace their descent through female members. When a Navajo baby is born he or she belongs to the clan of the mother and takes her clan name. When a young man marries it must be to someone completely outside his clan.

Families have rules to keep peace and order in their small dwellings. For example, because of the strong bond between mother and daughter, sometimes the relationship between a husband and his mother-in-law becomes tense. In past centuries a strict rule called the mother-in-law taboo existed among the tribes. According to the

A Navajo family poses outside a hogan, a one-room house built with logs and clay in which entire families often lived together.

taboo, a young man was never allowed to be in the same room with or address his mother-in-law, her sisters, or her mother. If a man and his mother-in-law needed to talk, a third person had to carry the message.

Living in a Hogan

In the past Navajo families lived together in large one-room houses called hogans. Today most Navajo live in more modern houses, and hogans are mostly used for ceremonies.

The Navajo build their hogans by digging a hole about two feet deep and twenty to thirty feet across. A framework of large logs is built to support the roof and walls. Smaller logs and poles, as well as brush, are piled up to make walls. A large hole is left in the center of the roof to admit light and allow smoke from the fireplace to escape. The door of the hogan is built on the east side of the structure in order to let in the light of the rising sun.

When the walls and roof are complete, the entire building is covered with several inches of clay, which is baked in the hot desert sun. These houses can be built in a day or two and will not leak except during long, hard rains, which are rare in the Four Corners region.

Outside the hogan Navajo families construct other important buildings. Corrals and pens are made to hold livestock. Open-sided sunshades, called *ramadas,* protect people from the hot sun when they work outside. Saunas, called sweat lodges, are used as places where people can gather socially and also perform important religious rituals.

In earlier times the entire family stayed inside the hogan when the weather was bad. Traditional Navajo families spent much of their day working outdoors, farming, preparing meals, sewing clothes, and making tools.

Food from the Land

The Navajo planted beans, squash, and corn together on mounds of dirt. These plants were called the three sisters because they help each other grow. The corn

A Navajo family shucks corn in a field. The Navajo use corn kernels to make tamales and other Navajo dishes.

supports the tendrils of the beans, and the beans return health-giving nutrients to the soil. The squash keeps most insects away, but its bright yellow flowers attract the helpful pollinating bee.

Red, yellow, and blue corn is the most important food in the Navajo tradition. The kernels of corn are often ground into a mush, wrapped in corn husks, and baked in the embers of a fire to make Navajo tamales. This bread, called kneeldown bread because a woman rested on her knees when making it, is like a hard cracker that can be stored for long periods.

This fry bread taco contains many of the same ingredients the Navajo cultivated. The tribe grew beans, squash, and corn on farms.

The Navajo also planted large orchards of peach trees, and for many years they gathered wild foods such as yucca fruit, prickly pears, pine nuts, and walnuts. They hunted deer, antelope, rabbits, prairie dogs, and other animals common to the Southwest. Later, the most popular meal was lamb stew and fry bread.

Shepherds and Weavers

While farming was important, by the 1700s the Navajo way of life revolved around the tribe's sheep herds. Almost every man and woman had at least a few sheep, and small children were given lambs to care for that would become part of the flocks in adulthood. Most families also kept angora goats. The fine, soft hair of these animals is called mohair and is used for weaving.

Older boys and girls cared for the sheep and goats, letting them out of the corrals early in the morning and driving them to pastures where they would eat grass all day. As evening fell children led the flocks back to the corral for the night. When the pastures around the hogan were eaten down to the ground by the hungry flocks, the family simply moved on to a new area and built another house.

The Navajo still raise sheep. Every year in spring the sheep are shorn of their thick winter coats of wool. Just as their ancestors did, Navajo women weave the wool into yarn and color it with vegetable dyes. Brown is made from the bark of alder trees, light gray from the berries of ironwood trees, and reddish purple from the roots of wild plum trees. This colored yarn is still used to make beautiful clothing, blankets, and rugs.

These items feature geometric designs that reflect the Navajo's environment. For example, symbols for lightning, clouds, desert mist, and rugged mountains are

A Navajo woman weaves wool into a blanket. The designs on the blanket symbolize different aspects of the Navajo's environment.

often woven into the designs. Weaving is difficult and time-consuming work. To make a rug three feet by five feet takes more than four hundred hours.

Beautiful Baskets

Navajo women also spend many long hours making beautiful baskets in the same way past generations did. Many of these baskets are for special occasions. For example, women make baskets for gifts when a couple gets married. These wedding baskets are considered **sacred** and are made of sweet-smelling sumac. Some strands of sumac are dyed a deep reddish brown with mountain mahogany root, juniper ashes, and black alder bark. Some are dyed black with tree sap from the piñon pine mixed with powdered coal.

Navajo women made these baskets using natural dyes for color and designs. Each creation holds a sacred meaning for the tribe.

Making a basket of this quality can take nearly a year, since sumac only grows in the spring and mountain mahogany can be collected only in the winter. Once the materials are assembled, a medium-sized basket twelve inches across can be woven by a skilled worker in about three months.

The patterns in baskets, like those in blankets, have special meaning. The black in the design symbolizes darkness, night, and rain clouds, and red is for the life-giving rays of sunshine. The hole in the center of the basket represents the beginning of life.

To the Navajo every basket, blanket, and ear of corn holds a sacred meaning. In this way the daily life of the tribe is filled with blessings from the gods, and the wonders of nature are woven into the fabric of their lives.

Chapter Three

Beliefs and Rituals

The Navajo are deeply spiritual people who cherish ancient religious beliefs. In Navajo ancient religion, water, sun, moon, skies, winds, plants, rocks, and animals are all alive with gods and goddesses. These deities are able to make the rains fall, ensure an abundant harvest, and help people live long and happy lives.

The Navajo honor their deities in dozens of ritual feasts and dances held throughout the year. Some of these last up to seven days and include chanted prayers, rhythmic drumming, elaborate costumes, frenzied dancing, and feasting. Behind the rituals is a deep respect for the natural world. The Navajo gods and goddesses are part of this world.

Four Sacred Mountains

The Navajo believe that their creator placed them on the land between four sacred mountains. These mark the four directions of their land—north, south, east, and west—and give their world a special beauty and harmony.

The Navajo believe that the Sacred Mountain of the East is Mount Blanca, near Alamosa, Colorado. The Sacred Mountain of the South is Mount Taylor, north of Laguna,

A Navajo dancer honors the gods in a ritual dance. The tribe holds feasts and ceremonies to revere the land and praise the gods.

New Mexico. The Sacred Mountain of the West is San Francisco Peaks, near Flagstaff, Arizona. And the Sacred Mountain of the North is Mount Hesperus in the La Plata Mountains of Colorado.

The Navajo believe that after the gods, or Holy People, put the sacred mountains in place, they put the Sun and the Moon into the sky. The Holy People also made all the other necessities of life, such as clouds, trees, animals, and rain.

Walking in Beauty

Inspired by the beauty of their surroundings, the Navajo model their lives on the perfection of nature. Their goal is to create harmony, happiness, and goodness, a state of being called *hozho*, the Navajo word for "walking in beauty."

Navajo medicine men stand outside their hogan with a patient (on crutch). Medicine men perform healing ceremonies for the tribe's sick.

Hozho can be interrupted by powerful forces that can cause harm or disorder. For example, people can fall under the influence of bad luck, ill health, or negative feelings such as thoughtlessness and cruelty. If this happens, religious rituals are performed to bring back the *hozho*. These ceremonies are known as **chantways**.

Chantways

Chantways are very complicated ceremonies that include long chants performed by singers. Some of the longest chantways take up to nine days to perform. The Navajo believe that the chantways, when conducted properly, attract the attention of the Holy People. If the chantways are performed correctly, the Navajo believe that the Holy People will cure the patient and restore *hozho*.

Different kinds of songs cure different kinds of illnesses. A ceremony called a Shootingway, for example, might be used to cure an illness caused by a snakebite,

Navajo men pose next to a medicine lodge where healing ceremonies will be performed. These ceremonies, also known as chantways, called on the gods to cure the sick.

Navajo elders are respected as wise members of the tribe. Elders keep the ancient rituals of the chantways alive.

lightning, or being shot by an arrow. A Lifeway may be sung to cure an illness caused by an accident. An Enemyway is said to heal illness caused by a curse from a non-Navajo.

Chantways have been passed from one generation to the next for thousands of years. Since they are so long and complex, no single person can remember more than one or two of the rituals. As a tribe, however, **elders** are able to teach dozens of chantways to young people. In this way, Navajo healers are able to sing away sickness and restore *hozho* with song.

Blessingways

Some chantways are performed to bring blessings, increase luck, and maintain good *hozho*. These ceremonies are called Blessingways. They are performed for many different occasions such as blessing new mothers or protecting warriors, families, crops, or flocks of sheep.

When a couple gets married, the Navajo bride is given a four-day Blessingway ceremony. The words to this long sung ritual contain advice about married life from many older, more experienced women. Each day after the ceremony, the bride-to-be runs a long distance, symbolically following in the footsteps of all the women who were married before her. This is a very happy event as the young woman is welcomed into the community of adults.

Community Prayer

Whenever a Blessingway is held, many friends and relatives come together for the ceremony. The hosts build shelters and prepare food for the visitors. They also pay the singers to chant. People talk, sing, feast, and exchange gifts.

The ceremonies usually start at sundown and continue nonstop for at least two nights and one day. On the first night everybody prays and sings together. The guest of honor holds a sacred **bundle** to his or her chest. This bundle contains soil from the tops of all four sacred mountains. Songs and prayers continue throughout the entire night, into the next day, and throughout at least one more night.

Such events attract large numbers of people who want to sing and pray to the Holy People to maintain *hozho*. The Navajo believe that everyone who participates is blessed by the Blessingway, and everyone who comes to watch the chantway brings good wishes for the person being healed. By singing and dancing and praying together, everyone who attends has more harmony, beauty, happiness, and goodness in their lives.

Sand Paintings

During the Navajo ceremonies singers may create several sacred pictures called sand paintings. These are made from sand colored with natural dyes. For example, yellow sand is made from sand and corn pollen, while black sand is sand dyed with charcoal that came from a lightning-struck tree.

Sand paintings are sacred forms of art made with sand and natural dyes. Healers create the paintings in a slow ritual designed to cure illness.

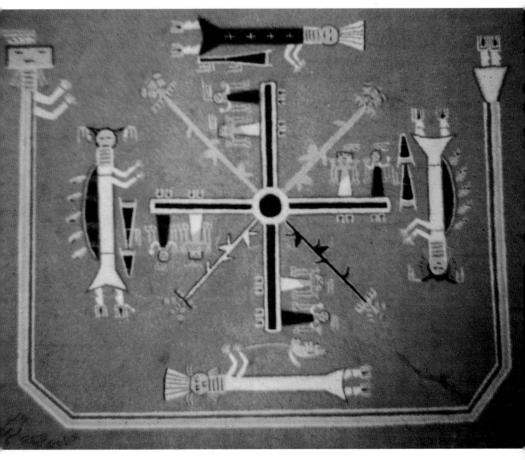

Like the chantways, sand paintings can take up to nine days to complete and are created by healers to restore *hozho* in a sick person. Sand painters create their healing artwork slowly, trickling the colored sands from their hands onto the floor of the patient's hogan. Subject matter may include images such as rainbows, lightning, mountains, and plants, along with images of the Holy People who are often shown traveling on rainbows.

The painters work out from the center, enclosing the sand painting in a circle from one to twenty feet across. The patient is placed inside the circle of the painting to receive the power of the Holy People.

At the end of the healing ceremony, the singer dips his hands in herbal medicine and places his wet palms on the dry powder of the painting. In this way the sacred figures of the Holy People and their healing tools are transferred onto the singer's palms. The singer then transfers the sacred images onto the body of the patient by laying his palms on the patient's skin.

After the patient is treated, others may come up to the sand painting and daub colors on themselves to bring harmony to their own lives. After the ceremony ends the sand painting is swept up and removed from the hogan floor.

The religious life of the Navajo, like their work lives, is a shared community experience. Everyone comes together to give blessings to the patient. In turn they also receive the blessings of the healing ceremony. This restores *hozho* to the entire community.

Chapter Four

Reservation Life

Over the centuries the Navajo way of life has undergone many changes. The tribe adopted parts of Pueblo and Spanish culture and often fought wars that forced them to move from place to place. When their desert homeland became part of the United States on February 2, 1848, the Navajo once again faced an uncertain future.

While the Navajo had been able to coexist with the Spanish, the American era quickly became one of the most tragic in their long history. American settlers flooded into the region. They hungered after the wealth of silver, gold, precious minerals, lumber, water, and other natural resources found there.

The U.S. government sent the army to take control of the new territories and confine the Navajo on a **reservation**. Any claims the tribe had on their ancient homeland were ignored. Meanwhile the Pueblo sided with the U.S. Army in order to get the lands back that the Navajo had taken from them.

With no one to help the Navajo resist, the U.S. Army built Fort Defiance in the heart of Navajo country in 1851. In the following decade, as U.S. Army horses and mules claimed more and more of the finest Navajo grazing lands and water sources, small battles broke out. In

A group of Navajo sits at the entrance to Fort Defiance. Navajo warriors attacked the fort in 1860 to drive the U.S. Army from the land.

April 1860 the tribe tried to drive the army out of their territory by attacking Fort Defiance with one thousand warriors. The Navajo almost overran the fort until American gunfire drove them off. Stung by the attack the Americans declared "total war" on the Navajo. In 1863 army officials ordered the defiant Navajo rounded up and imprisoned at Fort Sumner, an isolated military outpost in the east-central part of the territory.

The Long Walk

Despite fighting a losing battle, the Navajo refused to leave their homeland at Four Corners, so American soldiers destroyed all their dwellings, fruit trees, and crops, and shot all their horses and sheep. With no food and no place to live, more than eight thousand Navajo were rounded up and forced to walk more than 350 miles through spring blizzards to Fort Sumner. On the way more than three hundred Navajo died from disease or exhaustion, and others were shot by soldiers. This sad time for the Navajo people was called the Long Walk.

A young Navajo stands in the snow. During the Long Walk, the tribe was forced to march more than 350 miles to a reservation at Fort Sumner.

The reservation at Fort Sumner was too small to hold so many prisoners. The water was salty and the soil too poor to grow food. Many Navajo died of hunger, and thousands more were killed by an epidemic of smallpox. Finally, in 1867, the U.S. government Bureau of Indian Affairs (BIA) took over responsibility for the Navajo people from the U.S. Army.

In 1868 the BIA signed a treaty allowing the Navajo to return to part of their ancestral lands. Under the plan a reservation was set up that contained 3.5 million acres in the Four Corners region. The Navajo were given seeds and planting tools, along with thousands of sheep and goats and cows to graze on the reservation. But life would never be the same as it was before the Long Walk. Once rich and powerful the Navajo now were very poor.

The tribes were forced to adapt to many changes in their new home. On the reservation children were taken away from their families to live at boarding schools. They were taught to dress, act, and speak the language of American children. Navajo families also were surrounded by many American settlers who had moved onto the land while the Navajo were at Fort Sumner. Tribe members found themselves living in two very different worlds, one Navajo and the other American.

Trading Posts

By the early 1900s trading posts were scattered throughout the reservation. Navajo traders brought wool and food from their farms to trade for items such as cloth, flour, coffee, and metal goods. Seeing a growing interest in Navajo blankets, rugs, and baskets, traders sent catalogs out to merchants on the East Coast, advertising the colorful, creative work of Navajo weavers.

Another item in great demand was silver jewelry made by Navajo men. Before the Long Walk some Navajo had learned how to work silver from their Mexican neighbors. After the Navajo returned to the reservation, traders brought in Mexican jewelers to teach more Navajo men to make silver jewelry for trade. The traders also mined turquoise and brought it to the Navajo men

The Hubbell Trading Post opened in the 1800s and has been in continuous operation since.

A Navajo silversmith works on handmade jewelry. Silversmiths used turquoise and silver to create trinkets known as Navajo-style jewelry.

to set into their jewelry. The very popular turquoise and silver trinkets became known as Navajo-style jewelry.

Industry and Education

The flocks of sheep and goats increased, and once again the Navajo began to live well. But by the early 1930s, severe drought and overgrazing caused extreme hardships on the reservation. BIA agents tried to convince the Navajo people to sell off some of their sheep and goats, which were trampling the land and eating the grasses down to the dirt. Navajo families, however, depended on their sheep and goats to make a living. Farm animals were often used for trading instead of money.

Fights broke out and some Navajo people went to jail for fighting the agents and refusing to round up animals. Nonetheless, in the 1930s and 1940s, thousands of animals were sold off. This forced many Navajo shepherds to find jobs working elsewhere such as on the railroads, in factories and restaurants, or as servants.

In the 1940s many Navajo people had jobs working outside the reservation. When the United States entered

When their sheep ran out of grazing land, many Navajo searched for jobs outside the reservation. Some Navajo shepherds found work on the railroads.

World War II in 1942, thousands of Navajo men and women served their country in the military. Because the Navajo language could not be understood by the enemy, hundreds of Navajo were recruited by the U.S. Marines to send secret messages in their native language from the front lines to American leaders. Although the project was considered top secret for years, these Navajo "code talkers" were American heroes who were finally honored by the Department of Defense in 1992.

Two Navajo marines use their native language to send secret messages during World War II. Thousands of Navajo were recruited as "code talkers."

A Better Life

After the war most Navajo people did not have the skills they needed to find good jobs in mainstream society. To remedy this, in the 1950s the BIA set up thirty-six temporary schools in trailers scattered across the reservation. For the first time many Navajo children did not have to travel far away from their families and live at boarding schools. Now they could go to school during the day and return to their families at night.

The Navajo built about twenty more schools with money from their own lumber industry, as well as from American companies who paid them to mine oil, gas, coal, and uranium on the reservation. But the mines caused illness and pollution in the Navajo community. The Navajo people decided they needed to take more control of their own education to make better lives for themselves.

Two Worlds

In 1966 the tribes opened the Rough Rock Demonstration School to teach Navajo language, culture, and history. This school is run by local people who are elected by the Navajo population. The Rough Rock school publishes and distributes new educational tools such as a beginning reading book written in both Navajo and English. The stories in the book are drawn from real Navajo experiences and ancient stories of the Navajo people. Using these books teachers continue to encourage children to better understand their own culture as well as mainstream American society.

Rough Rock school became a model for other Navajo schools, which also began to teach Navajo ideas and values. Parents became more involved in the education of their children, and more Navajo became teachers

Navajo men play basketball on a reservation.

and helped to run the schools. In 1968 the Navajo established the first Native American college, now called Diné College. Today the college has small campuses in towns throughout the reservation.

Many Navajo people still speak their language, practice their ancient ceremonies, and honor the timeless values of their culture. But like most Americans they also watch TV, shop in malls, and work on computers. As the Navajo begin the twenty-first century, they continue to change and adapt to the conditions of living in two worlds. They believe that the wisdom of the past will help them to create a better future.

Glossary

adapt: To fit into a specific situation.

bundle: A group of sacred objects used in Native American religious ceremonies.

chantways: Ceremonial singing that uses the power of the human voice for healing sickness.

elder: An older, important member of a tribe.

hozho: A Navajo word meaning to live in harmony with everyone and everything.

mission: A building used by Christian missionaries who have come from a foreign land to carry on religious work.

nomadic: To move according to the seasons from place to place in search of food and water.

reservation: A tract of land set apart by the federal government for the use of Native American people.

sacred: Religious objects, ceremonies, or practices set apart for worship.

For Further Exploration

Sonia Bleeker, *The Navajo: Herders, Weavers, and Silversmiths.* New York: William Morrow, 1958. This is the story of Slim Runner, a Navajo boy on a modern reservation. The story is set in a rich background of true Navajo history and customs.

Virginia Hoffman, *Navajo Biographies.* Phoenix: Navajo Curriculum Center Press, 1974. The Navajo story as seen through the life stories of individuals.

Bruce Hucko, *A Rainbow at Night: The World in Words and Pictures by Navajo Children.* San Francisco: Chronicle, 1996. This book tells a story about traditional and modern Navajo culture through the paintings and drawings of Navajo children.

Andrew Santella, *A True Book: The Navajo.* New York: Childrens Press, 2002. This short history of the Navajo people describes their customs, their interactions with American settlers, and the many changes in their traditional way of life.

Virginia Driving Hawk Sneve, *A First Americans Book: The Navajos.* New York: Holiday House, 1993. This book tells about the history and culture of the Navajo people and includes words from traditional songs and poems.

Westridge Young Writers Workshop, *Kids Explore the Heritage of Western Native Americans.* Santa Fe, NM: John Muir, 1995. Written by kids for kids, this book uses real-life stories to tell about the history, culture, and everyday life of members of the Navajo and other nations.

Index

Picture Credits

In some credits the image call number is listed in parentheses after the page number on which the image appears.

Cover: The Denver Public Library, Western History Collection, William Pennington (X-33076)

© Bettmann/CORBIS, 14, 33, 38

© CORBIS, 15, 26

Corel, 20

Courtesy Colorado Historical Society, 16 (CHS-B511), 29 (CHS-X3027)

The Denver Public Library, Western History Collection, 17 (X-33088), 25 (X-33077)

The Denver Public Library, Western History Collection, Kohlberg and Hopkins, 27 (X-33087)

The Denver Public Library, Western History Collection, Timothy H. O'Sullivan, 32 (Z-1943)

The Denver Public Library, Western History Collection, William Pennington, 36 (X-33039)

© Kevin Fleming/CORBIS, 40

© Karen Tweedy-Holmes/CORBIS, 21

© George H.H. Huey/CORBIS, 35

© Hulton-Deutsch Collection/CORBIS, 37

© Catherine Karnow/CORBIS, 18

© North Wind Picture Archives, 9, 11

© Marilyn "Angel" Wynn/Nativestock, 8, 24

About the Authors

P.M. Boekhoff is an author of more than 25 nonfiction books for children. She has written about American history, science, and the lives of creative people. In addition Boekhoff is an artist who has created murals and theatrical scenics and illustrated many book covers. In her spare time she paints, draws, writes poetry, and studies herbal medicine.

Stuart A. Kallen is the author of more than 150 nonfiction books for children and young adults. He has written extensively about Native Americans and American history. In addition Kallen has written award-winning children's videos and television scripts. In his spare time Kallen is a singer/songwriter/guitarist in San Diego, California.